The Monster 'My' Brain Tumour

Marie L. Jones

Grosvenor House
Publishing Limited

This book is published by
Grosvenor House Publishing Ltd
Link House
140 The Broadway, Tolworth, Surrey, KT6 7HT.
www.grosvenorhousepublishing.co.uk

A CIP record for this book
is available from the British Library

Paperback ISBN 978-1-83615-565-2
eBook ISBN 978-1-83615-566-9

CONTENTS

This collection, titled "The Monster my Brain Tumour" brings together a series of poems that chronicle the deeply personal journey through the experience of having a brain tumour. Each poem reflects a unique moment, emotion, or revelation encountered along this path.

Author Marie L. Jones, through this anthology, offers an intimate glimpse into her deepest thoughts, culminating in a story that provides closure and perspective, finally ending with a collection that relate to her daily.

Preface

A short and sweet note of my
life before my brain tumour
'Medulloblastoma'
I thought my six wardrobes of
clothes were essential. My
numerous pairs of sandals,
shoes, heals, boots: must
have items. So much beautiful
jewellery, designer luggage
and handbags Oh and that
amazing sporty car, exotic
holidays and a big house!
Spending on all left-over wages,
credit cards, store cards, ...so
many 'friends' to go out and
party with, popping the cork
from the bottle after a week
of hard work.
I thought I was invincible....
Until I was promptly brought
back down to earth to face my
inevitable reality that was :
'The Monster - the Cancer'
growing in my brain!
Since then, I have spent many

hours writing the odd note and
creating a few poems week to
week and now after many years
I've ended up with this!!!
I hope you enjoy reading it
as much as I've enjoyed
writing it.
Writing this has made me realise that
those things I was talking about
were nice: but they were just
'things' Things that money 'can'
buy... Wow So beautiful and
fantastic! What I
now know is that - no amount
of money can buy your health,
a million pounds can't magic
away the many awful incurable
illnesses and diseases that the
human race all over the world
unfortunately, live and die with
every single day.
I can also tell that Love is not
for sale, love isn't something
that you purchase like
a packet of crisps from the shop,
'not' true love, love is something
that no amount of money can
buy. It is something so deep
inside, strong and priceless.

The Monster part I

Arriving on a breezy spring
morning, was one
lonely single seed,

In no time it exploded
then millions appeared

Monster worked hard sourcing
water for them to feed,

The seeds assembled at the table
and thunderously cheered.

Like a Dictator: he hypnotised
every single cell, to
follow him and only him

He monitored and trained them
intensely, preparing them
for his war

So arrogant, and so delighted
at never having to
move a single limb

He'd bellow out loud to
all of them
"PAIN! PAIN!
MORE! MORE!"

At that moment, rumbling like a
volcano her head
it began erupting

She had suffered tremors for
months, causing stiffness
to her neck

But today the red-hot lava began
to flow so painful
and repulsing

She phoned her surgery
feeling like a sunken
shipwreck

A minute later she requested a
home visit as there was
no way she could drive

Much later, she heard someone
knocking loudly on
her front door

A man with a very stern face
had arrived

He sat down, quickly retrieving
the prescription he'd
dropped on the floor

He was so clever and quick to
diagnose her as just being

'STRESSED'

After signing he put his pen back
in his pocket, wafting the
paper for her to take.

Feeling dreadful having not even
washed let alone dressed

She thanked him, and held her
hand out for him to shake

On the Doctors exit he pointed
to her car sat all alone
on her driveway

Maybe in his mind he was
telling it off for not
chauffeuring her

But in her own mind, she knew
exactly what he
wanted to say

She closed the door, closed
her eyes as everything
became a blur

During the next few months,
she suffered daily
with the most
punishing headaches

"Of course, **'STRESS'**" her
Divorce, Exams and
the house sale

Her exams were to be her future:
no room for any mistakes

So, she just took another pain
killer and tried her
best not to fail

During these months of dreadful
pain after being
diagnosed with
'STRESS'

The army had been ordered
to continue inflicting
maximum pain

Their attacks were vicious,
creating an absolute
catastrophic mess

Meanwhile the Dictator lay
back dreaming of his
successful amazing reign

The lava was intense and
worsened when the
cavalry was rapidly
deployed

The Dictator would shout,
ordering each soldier to
get into their tank

Trying so hard to rest, she had no
idea, that the Dictator was
planning to make her
permanently 'unemployed'

Morning arrived; she crossed her
fingers hoping today's
Doctor would be of
a higher rank

She opened the door, her
insides immediately
smiled,
'a new doctor'

They sat down, he said she was
'STRESSED!' he
advised her to
relax and rest

He did mention her 'car' parked
outside, which didn't come
to her as a major shocker

She just thanked him, took more
pain killers, hoped and
prayed for the best

Sat in his comfortable chair
waiting to celebrate his
inevitable victory

The Dictator was still not and
would never be
fully satisfied

He wanted her to suffer and
feel much more misery

His 'war' so far, was successful
becoming massively
amplified

He would sit at his desk, feet
up, rustling through
his many plans

He spent hours assessing
his decisions:
how he would finally
'finish' her,

He imagined himself standing
before his millions
of faithful fans

There would be thousands of
banners, flags and the
entire crowd shouting
"We love you Sir "

"Month eight arrived"

Every single day the volcanic
eruptions became
so catastrophic

The lava was rapidly increasing
in volume causing
a huge increase
in pressure

The Dictator remained busy
every day engrossed
in his favourite topic

He saw himself a genius thinking
nothing could ever
destroy his only pleasure

Every day the lava continued to
burn, causing her
head to explode

She just carried on as normal
trying her best to eliminate
any **'STRESS'**

"Get the exams passed, divorce
done! the house sold"

But unknown to her, the Dictator
had many more issues he
wanted to address

"Month nine"

An electrifying storm of thunder
and lightning
struck her head

The strike inflicted pain
impossible
for her to cope with
for much longer

She lay terrified as it clapped
loudly in her head,
flashing intensely
under her bed

It turned out that the Dictator
had provoked the storm
to become so
much stronger

She desperately needed a doctor
but couldn't face the
"STRESS" of it again!

Instead, she lay there enduring
the storm with a blanket
covering her face

She imagined answering the door,
'Another lecture!!'

causing so much more
unwelcome pain!

She wanted to go back in time, to
when everything travelled
at a much slower pace

That evening the troops managed
to demolish a table full
of food and water

The Dictator stood proudly
having_rewarded his
beloved army

But little did he know, he was
about to face some
competition, as a
worried lady had plans
to help her daughter

Her mother was insisting
for her to phone out
of hours immediately.
Barmy!

Ten minutes later, lights were
flashing outside of
her front door

Within no time she was lay
down flat, strapped
securely to a stretcher

Then a micro-second later she
could hear the
engine's loud roar

At that very moment the
Dictator was rudely
interrupted at a crucial
point in his lecture

In no time at all she was quickly
wheeled into A&E

Her head was now feeling
as mixed up as her
very old Rubik's cube

A lovely Doctor offered her
some medicine,
and she definitely
didn't disagree

Not long after, she was put into a
a big cold and very
noisy white tube

The End of Part I

Monster Continued

Intro

Now in hospital she was safe,
as the entire building
was covered by a
protective invisible shield

So, this now meant the dictator
had no access to
continue increasing
his awful yield

Monster part II

It was the middle of the night she
was awakened by a nurse
whispering "don't worry"

She was suddenly placed onto
another stretcher,
everything was happening
in such a hurry

A second later she was being
zoomed up a motorway,
heading for a very
magical residence

She could sense the wizards there
could help her by using
their true magnificence

The next morning the Sun shone
so bright and a variety of
doctors came to explore

They questioned her, prodded
her, then all walked
away unsure

For the next five weeks she
followed a regimental
daily pattern

An MRI scan, doctors, tablets,
far too much broccoli
and many visitors
carrying a lantern

Today, her thirtieth birthday, she
was surrounded by so
many balloons and just
lay helplessly in bed

Visitors popped in and out, but
she just wanted to
escape and hide in her
warm garden shed

Lots of cards and so many
presents were stacking
up on the chair

She remained grateful forcing a
smile, but she really
didn't care

Week 6 arrived, and a white
wizard appeared
at her bedside

He was clear and gentle with
his opinion that he
was about to provide

Did she just hear him say
"I' think you have a
brain tumour'???

She wanted to shout, "I' think
you've got a bad sense
of humour'!!!

A week later the white wizard
asked her to go home
and rest

It was Christmas eve, and she
was not feeling
anywhere near
her best

She arrived home that evening
with Mum carrying her
luggage from her 6-week
holiday

Welcomed by the wagging tails
of Oscar and Henri,
many massive hugs,
it just felt like yesterday

Christmas day was spent lying
down on the sofa
with a bad head

While Dad and Sis were
playing on the Wii

competing
head-to-head

The next few days went by with
everyone feeling so sad

Everyone except the Dictator:
devious and bad

But the Dictator was excited
to be back at his desk
arranging lots more
work for his soldiers

He spread them around her
brain with each team
carrying hundreds of
dark boulders

Every single day the boulders
created more and
more painful pressure

The Dictator smiled delightfully
feeling so much pleasure

It was New Year's Eve morning,
and the volcano was
heating up again

She was lying in her bed
wondering how much
more pain could
she possibly sustain

Oscar jumped up and lay gently
next to her placing his
paw on her hand

She smiled thinking of him at the
beach running to catch
his ball in the sand

The Dictator remained busy
working so hard to meet
his upcoming deadline's

Yelling at his soldiers to insure
he's all over tomorrow's
headlines

He tapped his stick on the screen
waiting impatiently for
it to be fully uploaded

Then raised his glass when his
volcano finally exploded

It was now late evening, and the
pain was excruciating
like never before

She lay there like a stone statue
wondering how much
more could she endure?

Then she opened her eyes to
see her mum was
sat next to her

There was also a doctor but
opening her eyes
to the lights was far
too painful for her

She was given a magical tablet,
and a porter took her
to a new magical ward

Within an hour her dream had
come true, the pain had
disappeared, so she
thanked the Lord

She felt more awake and alive
at that moment than
she had in her whole life

But then reality struck, and she
knew that soon she'd
be under the knife

The next morning, she was
transported back to
the magical land of
the White Wizard
and his clever team

She was given a room with an
en-suit wishing she could
just have a big bowl
strawberries and cream

Unfortunately, she was nil by
mouth for the entire day,
which made her
think more about food,
nothing but food

Today there was a continuous
flow of so many
people, all surprised
to see her in such a
happy mood

They were all full of good luck
wishes, lots of hugs and
so many kisses

She phoned and spoke to Oscar
and Henri telling them
how much she misses
(them)

She went to bed that evening
feeling so tired and
physically worn out

But she felt confident for
tomorrow,
she had no doubts

The Bad Day

She was up early showered, hair
washed and dried

Within minutes Mum, Dad,
Aunt and Uncle arrived

She reassured them that she was
going to be fine

And that she will be seeing them
again in no time

She was now joking with the
porter who was whizzing
her to the operation room

Having refused the 'pre-med' she
was just looking forward
to tomorrow's breakfast
room

Her nail varnish had already been
removed from her
fingers and toes

Before she knew it she was
counting one two three,
then began to doze

Seven hours later she was lying
on a big bed shivering
asking for a blanket

She was feeling so strange as if
she was on another planet

Then she was wheeled to a new
ward so that she could
begin to recover

Looking around, there were so
many beds filled,
she did discover

The first familiar face she saw
was the white wizard
and his blue eyes

Then mum and dad arrived,
smiling at her as if
they had won a prize

Her aunt and uncle were next
to see her, relieved
that she looked so well

Then she fell asleep, but was
woken and checked
at the sound of
every single bell

Then in the middle of the night
she opened her eyes
feeling so dreadful

She was in so much pain
throughout her entire
body it was so awful

She raised her arm, her fingers
touched the
back her head

It felt painful and numb both
at the same time,
she just wanted to be
in her own comfy bed

The following day was an
absolute car crash
as the anaesthetic
began to wear off

She cried non-stop, producing a
waterfall of tears that
could have filled a trough

Her uncle and cousin arrived and
held her hands, both
looking so very lost

Soon her mum and sister sat
down, she was still
crying but her fingers
were crossed

The following days weren't
too bad due to the
help of the magical
medicines

Considering she had a stapled
skull, but not many
more abrasions

She just wanted to eat and
carry on eating
everything all day,
every day

She'd never known such a need
for food, but she was
enjoying every single
mouthful come what May

The Sad Day

Intro
It was Sunday evening, and a
lovely friend arrived armed
with fries, burger, a drink,
paper and a pen. They sat
together downstairs close
to the hospital's reception
area and they began to
create a 'yes' 'no' chart
which she planned to use at the
meeting tomorrow morning.

The meeting
She sat down in the room with
her suitcase, her pen
and chart

Looking at all of us, the wizard
said 'Shall we start?'

He began, 'I have removed
your tumour to
microscopic level'

She was pleased hearing
that he had destroyed
that horrid devil

She looked at her chart then
asked, 'Is it cancer?'

He replied, 'Yes' in his ever-so
gentle manner

She ticked the chart whilst asking
the second question

'What is it called? Can you spell
that for me please'
hiding any tension

For the next few minutes, her
insides remained calm

He explained everything, as if
he was reading her palm

She would be exempt from
driving for the
next two years

She sat thinking of her
amazing car with
all those gears

You will need to decide if you
want to save your eggs

'EGGS' she thought! She just
wanted the cancer gone
and her muscles
back in her legs

Going forward every month you
will be scanned and
attend check-up
appointments

She'd already been through so
much, she prayed asking
God, 'If they could come
to some kind of
agreement?'

Suddenly, her ears pricked up
when she heard him say
'You will lose your hair'

That was the cherry on top of
the cake for her, was she
playing 'truth or dare?'

The meeting was approaching its
end, she felt as if she'd
been dragged through
a hedge backwards

It took all of her strength not
to shout and scream,
she knew she could
save all of the upset and
ranting for afterwards

Soon everybody shook hands,
exchanged greetings,

she walked away thinking
how can this possibly be
happening to her?

She couldn't believe that her life
as she knew it, was
quickly becoming
a complete blur

Dad and sis were the first to
depart, within no time
his tyres burnt rubber

She answered her phone, but
her words were a
collection of blubber

Then mum turned the key,
so upset not knowing
what to say.

She just sat their praying,
hoping tomorrow
will be a brighter day

The Mask

January 31st she was introduced
to a new magical building

She was led to a room where
many people
were busy working

She was asked to lie down flat
on a nearby bed

Then cream was rubbed all over
her face and head

She was fed up of lying down
she just wanted to run,
run away forever

But instead, her head was
placed in a clamp,
she had to surrender

She did feel uncomfortable,
but she didn't complain

She spotted tubs and was curious
about what they could
possibly contain

The artist to the right of her was
holding what looked like
a large pair of tweezers

She then gently placed strips of
paper onto her face
which felt so soft like
bird's feathers

The artist to the left of her took
out a spoon and what
looked like little trowel

He spooned out some plaster
and boy did he master
without even needing
a towel

Within a couple of hours, a dry
outstanding masterpiece
had been created

It was then carefully removed
from her face, when
she saw it, she was
ever so astounded

She felt a bit crazy still lay down
wearing those funny
goggles fixed to her nose

In seconds she was sat up having
her cheeks wiped which
shone like a red rose

February 7th she was invited
back to model her
very own tailor made
Halloween mask

It fitted perfectly but she felt a
bit smothered still
having so many
questions to ask

She arrived home that day ready
to drop, she closed her
eyes then fell to sleep

For the next six days she put on
her best smile and tried
so hard not weep

February 14th - for the next six
weeks, she was going
to be seriously tested

She'll be dressed in her very own
uniform ready to be
buckled up and belted

The Machine

Day 1
She woke, showered, dressed
then waited at the
window for Mum
to arrive

For the next hour she silently
gazed out of the car
window just letting
her mum drive

They arrived at the carpark
way too soon, she began
grinding her lovely white
teeth feeling so nervous

Now approaching the main
entrance her kind hands
became tight fists
enormously anxious

Marching, with mum hurrying
behind they followed the
signs to Radiotherapy

She waited at reception knowing
that this will soon
become her ordinary

Then sat in the waiting room,
she saw so many sad
looking people

No matter what age, colour,
gender, creed - sat there,
they were all equal

They were all sat there waiting
for the exact same thing,
'their turn in the machine'

For the next six weeks this was
going to be her
daily routine

Within half an hour she heard
her name being called
out loud

A kiss from her mum, then she
stood up proud

She was then led into what
looked like a
huge warehouse

She closed her eyes imagining,
that it was really a
beautiful manor house

She was then brought back to
reality being handed a
standard hospital gown

The changing room was dark
and cold, she felt like
she was about to drown

She was then placed on a big
cold, metal bed

Then she spotted the mask
created for her
delicate head

Next, the nurses safely secured
her to the metal table

So, if she needed to move, she
would be unable

Her ankles were the first to be
strapped, then her wrists

The mask was passed over as
they ticked their lists

Finally, it was gently placed
on her face

It was then screwed precisely
into table base

Next door a doctor was working
hard tapping on
his computer

Programming 'maximum dosage'
to the radiation diffuser

Before the button was pressed,
doors were closed when
everyone had vacated
the room

She was now alone in the dark,
feeling so lost and
full of gloom

She heard a noise, then a smell
making her feel sick

Soon the door was open, nurses
scurried back in so quick

Their job was to adjust direction
of the horrid blast

With changes complete they
exited very fast

Now, before the button was
pressed they'd shout
for her to hold her breath

Helping her a little, she lay
trying her best not
to think of death

The final blasts were for her
entire spine

She was told to conceal her
neck and back from

what is now
'dangerous' sunshine

Hearing that statement made it
hard for her to be
the perfect patient

Once the session was completed,
she was unstrapped
and set free

Within minutes, fully dressed,
and mum was ready
to turn the key

She couldn't move, or even think,
but she knew one thing
for sure, that she
was still alive

She knew deep down that, the
awful machine was going
to help her to survive

Day 1 - done and dusted
29 days to go and
a generous 6
weekends off, she knew
that these weeks were
going to be very difficult

She also knew that she had to
stay positive and fight
to get the best
possible result

Day10 arrived and she was
having a lovely warm
shower until she
looked down

The normal clean white shower
base had turned into
an ugly blonde brown!!!

She was shocked and angry.
muttering, 'no, not
now, this isn't allowed
to happen'

No not today she thought as
she grabbed her towel
with the pink pattern

She then grabbed her hair dryer
and tried to make the
best of such a mess

She managed to find a suitable
hat and then put on
her denim dress

She ran to her Mum's car, turned
the radio up, and didn't
speak one word, whilst
trying not to think about
her current sanity

Four hours later she arrived
home asking her mum
to help with her
current catastrophe

Her dad became a barber the
next morning and
did his worst with his
hair trimming gadget

She sat frozen on the chair
gritting her teeth,
whilst clinging on to
favourite blanket

She grabbed one of the scarves
that she had been gifted
then placed it on her
head securely

She then ran up to her bedroom
making sure it looked
pretty and fitted precisely

Dad was now transformed into
'Super Chef' and began
to prepare a scrumptious
lunch for his sad family

Soon mum and sis were sat down
at the dining room table,
while she just tapped
her nails so angrily

The Mirror

Every morning, she woke and
saw a stranger in her
mirror, sending a quiver
down her spine, she'd
whisper and bicker
then just give it the finger

The stranger's head was so bare,
she looked at it thinking
this isn't fair, she'd always
taken care of what was
once her beautiful hair.

The stranger's face was round
like the moon, it was
covered with tiny hairs
that required an urgent
prune, imagining she
was in a cartoon, there
was a balloon that will
take her up to meet Mr
spoon on Button moon

There was a scarf 'sickbay' right
next to her on display,
she just looked at their

beauty in dismay, she'd
delay choosing, feeling
each represented the
previous doomsday, when
she really wanted to
portray a celebration like,
'a birthday'

She began to recall the days when
she treated her hair like a
delicate lace, she'd style it
and embrace, never
having one strand out of
place completing her
happy smiling face

Looking deeper into the mirror
her cheeks had lost their
elegant chisel but had
gained a dimple, making
her feel a 'tad' dismal
having lost their twinkle,
they looked sad, plain
and simple

Her and her mirror eventually
became friends, after
such an upsetting time
of hating and rejecting
each other she began

accepting this new
vision, welcoming it
into her new life.

She didn't realise until years
later that the medicines
she thought were
destroying her, were
assisting the repair of
her body, disposing
of all the rubbish,
discarding the pain,
allowing for a new
beginning of rejoicing a
second chance at life

The Years

For many years I just couldn't
accept

I floated around feeling
like a reject!

For many years I grieved
heavily for you

Everywhere I ventured I
had no idea of
'Who was who'

For many years I found
a new job after
another new job

With no exceptions I'd
repeatedly fail
and deeply sob

For many years I was
told that everything
was going to be fine

But nobody told me that
I would probably
decline

For many years I dreamed
of destroying that
devil of a machine

It demolished my brain
leaving me feeling
angrily green

For many years I hoped
for you to come
back home

You'd help me remember,
then seal the hole

For many years I was
drowning in
my own tears

Feeling anxious about
the future, causing
me so many fears

For many years I was
hopelessly lost

"I FOUGHT FOR YOU !!"
but at what cost!

For many years I despised
the 'new me'

I often clenched my teeth
thinking
"how can this be?"

For many years I prayed
endlessly for you
to come back

But as time passed by, my
faith began to lack

For many years I longed for
what was once
'my beautiful hair'
to come back to me

I conjured up every spell in
my head, but the
machine had
turned its key

For many years I woke up
shouting
"THIS ISN'T FAIR"

I was expecting a miracle,
but you didn't care

For many years I was so
critical and always
disappointed
with myself

I battled monotonously
but always slipped
off the shelf

For many years I detested
my 'new' brain,
always forgetting this
and always forgetting
that

In this 'new' world I was
repeatedly failing
so, I'd apologise
profusely then
hand in my hat

For many years I should
have been recording
and noting
every day

I'd wake up happy, only to
be upset by the
inability to
remember the
previous day

For many years I hated
feeling that I was
no longer complete

Did you just pack a bag
and drift away, after
pressing delete?

Finally, for many, many,
years, I am proud
that I have always
tried to keep
a smile on my face

I always hope that one day
I will get a trophy
when I eventually
'WIN' this race

Choice

I wasn't given a choice when
a bomb was placed
in my brain

A clock ticking non-stop
causing me so much
horrendous pain

There was no way of controlling
this explosion in my head

The radiation attacked so many
cells, just leaving
them for dead

I had no choice when it came
to my daily memories
being deleted forever

But just because I don't
remember things,
doesn't make me
any less clever

The things I can choose, is to
accept that, everything
happens for a reason

For so many years I wasted time
wishing for the arrival
of the next season

Eventually I chose to accept and
enjoy this new life that
I have been gifted

Every single day that I wake up,
I dress,
I smile,
always feeling lifted

I choose to love every second
of every day for as
long as I am alive

The only thing that I wish for
every night, is that
tomorrow will arrive.

Acceptance

After many years of trying so
hard with absolutely every
single thing in my life

And so many years of battling
endlessly with my newly
damaged brain

After many years of despising the
forgetfulness that I have
been lumbered with

And so many years of failing at
every single job that
I attempted

After many years of having to
make excuses for my
many never-ending
mistakes

And so many years of adjusting
to this inconvenient
limited concentration
span

After many years of always feeling
tired and having to
constantly apologise

And so many years of wishing
that one day I will
wake up and it was
all just a bad dream

After many years of having to
endure dreadful
financial trauma

And so many years of worrying
and stressing about
every single headache

After many years of suffering
with depression and
having random
anxiety attacks

And so many years of being
filled with so much
confusion, I finally
began to accept

'These days' I have learned to
empty my mind of
every negative thought

I have come to realise that I no
longer need to crunch
numbers like I was taught

I no longer make excuses for my
guaranteed daily mishaps

Instead, I proudly hold my head
high, smile and maybe
take the odd cat nap

'These' days, I feel content with
myself in this new world
I have found

I see so much with my bless 'ed
eyes and try my best to
listen to every single sound

I enjoy many adventures with my
fluffy baby girl safely
on her pink lead!

I'm so grateful for every bit of
help and support that has
enabled me to succeed

My Love

Having avoided death; I appreciate
every single breath
that I inhale into
my body's deepest depth.

I always wish that tomorrow will
arrive so, when I wake
up and my brain is still
alive, me and my dog
share a happy hi-five.

I love the sky's darkness, but I also
admire the moons slice
of brightness and then I
imagine the stars magically
appearing on my canvas.

Always loving the Autumnal
changing of the leaves,
but not loving the frosty
morning breeze
that makes my toes freeze.

I love watching the rain drops
falling, hearing the crows
calling seeing the puddles
forming

I love travelling on the train, I find
looking out of the window
rests my brain, it's much
better than driving and
stressing over which lane.

I love it when Spring opens
the frozen tomb,
encouraging a mass of
beautiful flowers to
awaken and bloom, which
attract the butterflies to
flutter around leaving no
room for any gloom

I love that I now love my new hair,
I love the wind blowing in
my new hair,
if it gets blown out of style
I really don't care

I love the beauty of the vast city
with all its hustle and
bustle, but love coming
home to the fresh
countryside's open space
without having to shuffle

I love chocolate, so smooth and
creamy, delicious and

dreamy, but sometimes
I have to say no! you're
making me so very greedy

I love my family, and friends that
aren't family, but I always
welcome them into my
family, especially my dog
she is the head of my
family
(don't tell my Dad I said that)

I love the nearby river which is
brought to life by the
nearby castle both being
either side of the beautiful
nearby church

I love every genre of music, music
never fails to lift me up so
high, even higher than
the sky, so high that I
feel that I could fly

I love snooker, I am literally
snooker loopy
'mesmerised'
by Ronnie, when he's
at the table there's
no time for a coffee,

I just watch him cue
and enjoy my ice
cream banoffee

I love creating beautiful things,
especially everything
that is still familiar,
including the artwork
that I paint, my delicate
embroidery and the
warm blankets that
I gently crochet

I love the sunshine during the
summer weeks, it
brightens the colour
of my cheeks and
miraculously awakens
the mountain peaks

I love the sensation of walking
bare footed in the sand,
listening to the waves
crash on to the land,
wishing for someone
to hold my hand

I love and cherish everything
in my life. I choose love and
happiness in my life, and
there's always room for more,
and more forever more.

Me Now

Having shared my story by literally extracting what was the worst time of my life, I'm now going to invite you into my new life. Believe me, it's not perfect but I love every second of it. There is life after tragedy. There is always hope.

There is always someone there to help you, listen to you, love you, or just give you a big hug. I know that because I never feel alone.

Well, that might be a little porky pie, because I do get the odd day when I feel a bit low or anxious, useless, alone, cold in a horrible dark place: but I've come to believe and know that tomorrow will be brighter, because it has to be. It has no choice, I can't waste another day feeling so dreadful, so I switch on my never-ending determination, make myself stand at the backdoor no matter what the weather is doing.

I'll breath in the amazing fresh air that we are blessed with, in through my nose and out through my mouth several times. I'll switch on my radio, listen to happy, uplifting music, and start my new day with a smile on my face. I'll be honest there is no magic formula, some days it's not that easy, the odd day there may be tears, but every day is my day. That may sound selfish, but I love my new-found independence. I make my own decisions and listen to advice from others, but nobody controls me and tells me what to do. I am my own person, a happy person. This new brain I have been gifted with is so special and I love it so much. I love that I can still walk my dog, 'Daisy'.

She is the love of my life, and there isn't a word to describe the amount of happiness she gives me. I tell her and everyone with whom I am blessed to tell 'I LOVE YOU'

I have my many friends and
family members that I am in
contact with. It could be an email,
text message, phone call, or meet
up for lunch or a cuppa. I feel
that I am the luckiest and happiest
person in the world

Just a Touch of Forgetfulness

Do you remember when we met
last week-

No, I don't, but I'm imagining
that we did speak!

Did you have a nice day today?

Yes, I think so, yes, why,
is it my birthday?

I can see the keys hanging from
the lock of the front door

It's early and for the life of me
I can't think what I would
have opened it for!

We spoke just ten minutes ago!
I told you I'll be getting
to yours for five.

Oh yes, I can see your email!
and text! telling
me when you're
going to arrive!

Did you enjoy your meal last night?
What did you have?

Yes, we all had such a laugh

Do you remember what I whispered
to you the other day?

Sorry, I'm a little short of hearing,
what did you say?

So how did yesterday's hospital
appointment go?

I can't remember
I don't know!

I want to talk to you about that
secret I told you.

Er... I think I might be having an
episode of déjà vu

Did you see that awful fire on the
news last night?

I think so, that one caused
by the moonlight?

Where were you yesterday,
we had a great
time out of town?

I forgot again. I'm so sorry for
letting you down

What did you think of that movie
you went to watch?

What are you talking about, have
you been on the Scotch?

You said that you liked the present
that I gave you?

Oh! Yes, I loved it thank you; would
you like a brew?

Ok we'll meet you there in
half an hour!

Two hours later 'I think my
Tom-Tom
ran out of power'

Well, I wouldn't be me if I
remembered
entirely everything!!!!!

I always loved my goldfish who had
a similar brain to me. 'Fred'
named after my Grandad

Loss of Politeness

Do you like my new hairstyle?

I think trying my hairdressers
might be worthwhile

I like mine; I've been going to mine
for years

Sorry, I meant to say
'I love your new hairstyle'

What do you think?
I think I'm losing weight,

Haha are you joking
after what you just ate!

Well yesterday you saw me squeeze
through your garden gate

Of course, my lovely I can see
you've lost weight

Oh, I love singing to this song

Please, please stop singing along!

Are you in a mood?
Did I do something wrong?

No, don't be silly I love that song

What do you think of this dress?

Well, I hope you're not wearing it
to impress?

Oh, this event is causing me
so much stress!

You'll be fine my friend you look
beautiful in any dress

I think he's gorgeous looking

Please stop all that swooshing

Oh well I can carry on wishing

You might not need to wish,
don't react but
he's looking

Do you like my new eyeshadow?

Why are you planning to
perform at panto?

Should I try one that's a bit
more mellow?

I think mellow will be your
perfect eyeshadow

Excuse me

Two of my most spoken words

Excuse me, do you work here?

Yes, I do, how may I
help you my dear?

Excuse me, you need to
join the que

And justtt who... are youuu?

Excuse me, I think you
dropped this?

Oh, thank you my lovely,
I could give you a kiss.

Excuse me, but you shouldn't
think like that!

I'll think wot I wanna think ye ol bat

Excuse me, could I get passed
you please?

Of course, it's just a little squeeze.

Excuse me, I'm sorry but I'm trying
to concentrate here,

Oh. Just get a pair of them plugs
and stick um in ye ear!

Excuse me, you, yes you,
where did you get that
beautiful blouse?

I can't remember, online probably,
I often browse.

Excuse me, that's my chair,
I was sat there,

Oh, I must apologise would you
mind if we share?!

Excuse me, excuse me, Excuse me,

Are you talking to me???

Oh, oh, oh, you must excuse me.

EXCUSE ME - Excuse - synonym -
1. Please excuse me, forgive, pardon

Please

Thinking you can do whatever
you please!

But you know how much
I love to tease

Please could you assist
me with this?

Of course, I'll do my very
best for you Miss

As you please...

I know how you like
to feel at ease

Oh please don't look at
it like that

Well, it was you that
mentioned it in
our last chat

I think I'll have a nice cup
of tea please

It will warm me up from
the outdoor freeze

It's always a pleasure to
please people

To make someone smile,
is like the sweet
taste of treacle

Yummy Yum Yum

A Star

Before you close your
curtains tonight

Look up to the sky and
you will see a star
shining so bright

Continue observing its
beauty, try your
hardest not to blink

You'll then see it smiling,
giving you a
cheeky wink

Then when you are warm
and cosy in your bed

The magical silver star dust
will caress your
sleepy head

There will be no darkness
in your dreams
tonight

You'll wake up in the
morning feeling
incredibly fresh
and bright

Dreams

It's 7pm and she's tired after
such a busy day
of nonstop play

Spent forever jumping around
chasing a big black fly

All along it was just teasing her
and disappeared into
the morning sky

She visited her friend Rupert
who lives near by

They played in his garden,
never wanting
to say goodbye

Now arriving home after her
lovely evening walk

She ran to her water bowl
with no time to talk

Before she knew it, her head
sunk into a cushion
as she curled up
on the rocking chair

Watching a movie with mum,
they make a lovely
perfect pair

10pm in the garden searching
for a place to
do her last wee

Now almost finished she's
counting 1 2 3

She then makes for the
stairs landing on
her fluffy bed

Then comes the softest
tummy rub
and her pink ted

Bedtime biscuits she munches
and sniffs out
the crumbs

She licks her lips, fingers
and thumbs

Drifting to sleep she dreams
of the beach

Her feet in the sand running
out of reach

Then quickly she returns
and asks for her ball

She runs towards the waves
only to find a waterfall

Mesmerised by this huge,
amazing water shower

She blinks and she's now
in the woods talking
to a little purple flower

Before she knows it, there
stands Sky, her gentle
equine friend

The love they share will
never end

She's now with Rupert playing
together as it snows

Then she spots the lady
holding the hair
dryer as her fur blows

Suddenly awakened from her
glorious dream

She sees her Mummy in the
morning sun beam

Now stood up with eyes wide
open and her ears
up in the air

She wakes up her Mummy
with her magical glare

In no time she's downstairs
thinking and knowing
as she takes a seat

Licking her lips, wagging her
tail, she gracefully
waits for her early
morning treat

Fluffy Girl

Brushed in the wind her
hair blows

Covering the pavement like
when it snows

A bird appears and creates
a clear patch

She then quickly flies off
to warm her hatch

The River Walk

She finally arrived at the big
metal gate

Repeatedly jumping up, with
no patience to wait

With her tail wagging, her eyes
so bright and finally,
her lead removed,

She then takes flight as her
sense of smell becomes
hugely improved

She sniffs every blade of grass
always leaving her
scent behind

She continues by tip toeing
along the pathway
which is so exquisitely
designed

To her left several swans' float
by with a beautiful air
of pure elegance

She pauses to watch them
gracefully display
true royal excellence

She walks further along the
pathway loving the
freshness of the air

She follows two butterflies,
dancing like a true
romantic pair

Then she hears the boisterous
quacking ducks
splashing and
chattering away

They appear to be a big happy
family enjoying every
moment of the day

She looks up to the sky to see
starlings performing
their classical dance

Tens of tiny ballerinas dancing
in sync with each
other sending her
into a trance

A little further along she spots
two people wearing
hats sat on a tweed
blanket

Within a second, she is
awakened sprinting
towards the scent
of the food in their
basket

In no time at all 'two' had
become a perfect
gathering of 'three'

She licks her lips whilst sitting
comfortably on the
gentleman's knee

The couple were smiling in
adoration of this
beautiful ever so
well-mannered baby

The couple then wished her
goodbye with a big
hug from the lady

Hearing that familiar whistle,
she heads back
wanting to play ball

For the next ten minutes
she is back and
forth to every call

She now approaches the
second metal gate
and shouts for
it to open

Waiting patiently, she hopes
birds hear how she is
so gracefully spoken

She then continues exploring
on her ever enjoyable
daily trek

She spots the sparrows ahead
and listens to their
every single peck

A touch further to the other
side of the pathway
are many rich
green fields

With the exception of one which
is a mass of bright
yellow yields

She woofs hello to the cows
wandering around

enjoying the luscious
green grass

Then waves to the sheep in
the field next-door,
with no time to stop
she must dash

Further along the path she
smiles seeing the
annual migration
of Canadian geese

With ears peaked and head
turning she remains
silent so not to
disturb their peace

She continues walking thinking
to herself what
a lovely day

Looking back to see her
mummy going the
opposite way

She panics and runs so fast
to catch up
with her mum

Shouting I've missed you
with her heart

beating as loud as
a big base drum

Now back on her lead and
a little bit tired they
both head for home

Licking her lips she knows
that her dinner will
soon be served in
her big pink bowl.

Daisy

She sniffs, I chat
She wee's, I wait
She runs, I smile
She barks, I look
She lays, I stroke
She howls, I sing
She jumps, I duck
She poo's, I bag
She burps, I laugh
She sleeps, I snore
She wakes, I give her massive
cuddles and kisses

Basically

I chose the following poem to end this part
of my story because it does make me
laugh and I hope it makes you laugh too
Basically, every single thing, that I say or do,
'well, they just happen?' - obviously without
my permission!
My excuse for using certain words so often is,
well, 'Basically' it's not 'my' fault, it's my faulty
brain.

Basically

Well basically it's straight
forward, you
just tap there

It's basically down that
corridor there then
up the first stair

Well basically it's not rocket
science, calm down,
don't have a mare!

Basically, I don't remember,
and I really don't care

Well basically, stop moaning
and sit on that chair

It's basically between three
dresses, which one
do I choose to wear

Well basically, don't you dare
look at me with
that awful glare

Basically, open that box of
chocolates right
now and share

Well basically, you returned
it, so I reckon
we're square
[thumbs up]

It's basically soft like a cuddle
from big brown bear

Well basically you should act
now, there's no
time to spare

Basically, it is as it is, what
you read is so
very rare

Well, 'basically 'a friend looked it up after my 'comedian' sister made me aware of how often I use this word. It just jumps out of my mouth and she basically laughs hysterically and repeats it every single time, I say it?!

BASICALLY

- adverb = can have two meanings

1. A pause in the speaker's conversation, giving them time to draw their breath.
2. A phrase used to illustrate the speaker in panic mode, while they think of what to say next.

Acknowledgements

I would like to thank 'all' of
my family and friends who
have helped, loved and
supported me on my journey,
endured my tears and worries
past and present. So, so many,
amazing caring people
'you all know who you are'.

I would like to make a special
thank you to two very special
gentlemen and their teams.

Without these amazing Wizards
I wouldn't be here today 18
years later to tell this tale.

The White Wizard
- Professor Andrew Brodbelt
Neurosurgeon
The Walton Centre

The mask/machine Wizard
- Dr Brian Haylock
Neuro-oncologist
Clatterbridge Hospital

A final deserved thank you to my Mum, for driving miles to visit me in hospital every single day, then driving back and forth every day to Clatterbridge. Then for the following two years becoming my chauffer taking me to all my various appointments and spoiling me with many lovely days out, managing to fit all of this in, whilst still having to work and put up with my very unpredictable moods.

Thank you to everyone who has
been on this journey with me,
joined my journey and still on
this magical journey

www.ingramcontent.com/pod-product-compliance
Ingram Content Group UK Ltd.
Pitfield, Milton Keynes, MK11 3LW, UK
UKHW040850260126
467307UK00001B/2

9 781836 155652